The College Cookbook

Dorm-Friendly Microwave and Mug Recipes

BY: Matthew Goods

Copyright Page

Table of Contents

Introduction

College students often pile on the pounds during their first and second year of studies, and it's all down to diet and poor eating habits.

So, forget fast food, ready-meals, and boring, bland dining hall food, and instead whip up dorm-friendly recipes to keep your belly satisfied and your brain focused.

But preparing food in a dorm can be a real challenge. All you may have is a microwave, toaster, and mini-fridge. Worse still, work and store cupboard space is most likely going to be pretty limited. The good news is, though, that doesn't mean you can't prepare budget dorm-friendly meals and snacks for yourself and even your roommates.

What's more, all you need - apart from a microwave, of course - is a mug, bowl, and some basic kitchen utensils. Better yet, no cooking skills are required!

Are you missing home-cooked meals? Don't stress, these 40 dorm-friendly microwave and mug recipes will help you create tasty mains, study snacks, sweet treats, and desserts. They take minimal effort to prepare, and you don't even have to leave your dorm!

Meals and Savory Snacks

BBQ Chicken Nachos

Forget that calorific take-out and instead opt for this dorm-friendly recipe. All you need is a bowl, plate, a little cutlery and, of course, a microwave.

Servings: 2

Total Time: 3mins

Ingredients:

- 1 cup rotisserie chicken (shredded)
- 3 tbsp BBQ sauce (store-bought)
- 2 large handfuls of tortilla chips
- 1 cup Cheddar cheese (shredded)
- ¼ cup pico de gallo
- ¼ cup scallions (thinly sliced)
- Guacamole (as needed, to serve)
- Sour cream (as needed, to serve)

Directions:

In a bowl, combine the shredded chicken with the BBQ sauce.

In a layer, add the tortilla chips to a microwave-safe plate.

Spread the chicken mixture over the tortilla chips, followed by a layer of shredded Cheddar, pico de gallo, and scallions.

Microwave the nachos on full power for around 1-3 minutes, until the cheese bubbles and melts.

Remove from the microwave, and serve with a dollop each of guacamole and sour cream.

Chicken Curry for One

If you live in a small space, don't have a lot of cupboard space, but crave a homemade curry, this simple recipe is the one for you.

Servings: 1

Total Time: 10mins

Ingredients:

- 1 tsp butter
- ½ onion (peeled and finely diced)
- 1 tbsp oil
- 1 cup cooked chicken breast (diced)
- 7 ounces tomatoes (chopped)
- 1 tbsp curry paste
- Salt and freshly ground black pepper (to season)
- Cilantro (chopped, to serve, optional)

Directions:

Melt the butter in a microwave-safe bowl for 10-30 seconds.

Add the onions and oil and mix thoroughly to combine. Return the bowl to the microwave for 30-60 seconds.

Add the diced chicken to the bowl, and cover tightly with kitchen wrap. Using a fork, pierce 3-4 holes in the surface of the wrap.

Microwave on full power, for 5-10 minutes, until the chicken is just cooked through.

Next, add the chopped tomatoes and curry paste. Season the curry with salt and black pepper, and mix well to combine.

Remove the bowl from the microwave and set aside to stand for 2-3 minutes.

Garnish with cilantro, if using, and enjoy.

Chicken Quesadilla

Tasty snacks that are quick to prepare are the key to study success, and these microwave chicken quesadillas will tick all the boxes.

Servings: 1

Total Time 4mins

Ingredients:

- 2 medium flour tortillas
- ½ cup cooked chicken (cut into strips)
- ½ red or green bell pepper (diced)
- 1 tbsp taco seasoning
- ¼ cup Cheddar cheese (shredded)

Directions:

Place the flour tortillas on a microwave-safe plate and microwave at full power until slightly crisp. Remove from the microwave, and allow them to dry out as they cool.

In a bowl, combine the chicken, bell pepper, and taco seasoning until fully incorporated. Cook in the microwave for 1-2 minutes until the bell pepper is softened.

Spread the chicken evenly over one tortilla, and cover with shredded cheese. Top with the remaining tortilla.

Cook for an additional 30-60 seconds, and enjoy.

Chicken Teriyaki

Serve chicken teriyaki as a filling for a wrap or bun and enjoy as a snack. Alternatively, elevate it to a main meal by serving it on a bed of rice or noodles with lots of healthy veggies.

Servings: 1

Total Time: 10mins

Ingredients:

- ¼ cup soy sauce
- 1 tbsp ketchup
- 2 tbsp garlic powder
- 6 tsp white sugar
- 1 boneless and skinless chicken breast half (cut into strips)

Directions:

In a bowl, combine the soy sauce with ketchup, garlic powder, and white sugar.

Add the chicken strips to the bowl, and toss to coat.

Transfer the coated chicken to a microwave-safe plate.

Cover with kitchen wrap and cook in the microwave on high for 5-8 minutes, until the chicken is cooked through.

Classic Chili con Carne

If you are planning a study break with fellow students, this classic chili will keep everyone on task.

Servings: 4

Total Time: 12mins

Ingredients:

- 1 pound ground beef
- 1 medium onion (peeled and finely chopped)
- 2 (14½ ounces) cans stewed tomatoes
- 2 tsp chili powder
- 1½ tsp prepared mustard
- 1 (15½ ounces) can kidney beans (rinsed and drained)
- Salt and freshly ground black pepper (to season)
- Cheesed (grated, as needed, to serve, optional)

Directions:

Crumble the beef into an 8-cup capacity microwave-safe bowl.

Add the onion, and mix thoroughly.

Cover with a lid and microwave on full power for 3 minutes, until the meat is no longer pink. Remove the cover, drain well and stir in the tomatoes, chili powder, and mustard, mixing well to combine.

Cover the bowl, and on high, microwave for 6-7 minutes.

Add the kidney beans and mix to combine. Cover once more and on high power microwave for another 2 minutes.

Season with salt and black pepper, garnish with grated cheese and enjoy.

Corned Beef

Corned beef is a really versatile dish. You can serve it as a sandwich filling, with creamy mash, or on a bed of veggies; the choice is yours.

Servings: 3-6

Total Time: 40mins

Ingredients:

- 1 pound 10 ounces corned beef
- 1 tbsp brown sugar
- 1 small onion (peeled and quartered)
- ⅛ cup white vinegar
- 1 cup water
- ½ tsp whole cloves (optional)
- 6 dinner rolls (split)
- Mustard or horseradish (to serve, as needed, optional)

Directions:

Add the corned beef to a microwave-safe dish. Add the sugar, onion, white vinegar, water, and cloves (if using). Stir to combine.

Cover the dish and cook on high power for 10 minutes.

Turn the microwave down to moderately high heat and cook for an additional 15 minutes.

Flip the meat over and cook for around 15 minutes.

Serve inside dinner rolls, add a dollop of mustard or horseradish and enjoy.

Egg and Cheese Muffin

Ditch the dining plan and make the most out of your microwave. This egg and cheese muffin is the perfect way to begin or end the day.

Servings: 1

Total Time: 3mins

Ingredients:

- 1 tsp butter
- 1 large egg
- 1 tbsp milk
- 1 dash of hot sauce
- 1 tbsp onion (peeled and diced)
- 1 English muffin (split, toasted, and buttered)
- 1 American cheese slice

Directions:

In a microwave-safe container, melt the butter for 10-15 seconds.

Add the egg to the butter and beat thoroughly.

Stir in the milk, hot sauce, and onion.

Cover the container with a kitchen paper towel and on high, microwave for 90 seconds.

Serve the egg inside a toasted and buttered English muffin, top with a slice of American cheese, and serve.

Faux-Fried Rice

Go wok-free and prepare this fabulous faux-fried rice in your trusty microwave.

Servings: 1

Total Time: 8mins

Ingredients:

- ½ cup rice
- 1 tbsp soy sauce
- 1 cup water
- 1 tsp sesame oil
- 2 bacon slices (chopped)
- ½ cup frozen peas and carrot
- 2 eggs
- Salt (to season)
- 1 tbsp fresh scallions (to garnish)

Directions:

In a microwave-safe bowl, combine the rice with soy sauce, water, sesame oil, and chopped bacon Stir to combine and covered, on high, microwave for 6-8 minutes, or until the rice is cooked.

Add the frozen veggies to the rice, and stir to combine.

In a microwave-safe mug, beat the eggs and season with salt.

Cook the eggs in the microwave until cooked through. Break the eggs up into small pieces, stir into the rice, garnish with scallions and enjoy.

Four-Minute Mac and Cheese

Easy, cheesy, and guaranteed to please pasta-lovers everywhere, this mouth-watering mac and cheese is sure to become your go-to dorm-friendly meal in a mug.

Servings: 1

Total Time: 4mins

Ingredients:

- ½ cup water
- ½ cup elbow macaroni
- Salt (to season)
- 3 tbsp milk
- ¼ cup Cheddar cheese (shredded)
- Black pepper (to season)
- Fresh chives (chopped, to garnish)

Directions:

In a microwave-safe mug, combine the water and macaroni. Season with salt and stir to combine. Microwave on high for 2-3 minutes, and stir.

Add the milk, shredded Cheddar, and season with salt and black pepper. Stir once again to combine.

Microwave on high power for an additional 30 seconds, stir well, and if using, garnish with chives.

Greek Whole Grain Brown and Wild Rice Bountiful Bowls

They say that the Mediterranean diet is one of the healthiest in the world, so when you need to concentrate, it makes sense to include this bountiful rice bowl in your weekly meal plan.

Servings: 2

Total Time: 12mins

Ingredients:

- 1 (8 ounces) package ready-to-serve brown and wild rice medley
- ¼ cup Greek vinaigrette (divided)
- ½ ripe avocado (peeled, pitted, and sliced)
- ⅔ cup grape tomatoes (halved)
- ¼ cup feta cheese (crumbled)
- ¼ cup Kalamata olives (pitted and sliced)

Directions:

In a microwave-safe bowl, combine the rice medley with 1 tablespoon of vinaigrette. Cover the bowl and on high, cook for around 2 minutes, or until heated through.

Divide the rice mixture between 2 individual salad bowls.

Top with slices of avocado and tomatoes.

Scatter over the crumbled feta cheese and sliced olives.

Drizzle over the remaining vinaigrette.

Loaded Potato

There are few dishes as filling as a loaded potato. And the good news is when you have a microwave, you don't even need a stove!

Servings: 1

Total Time: 9mins

Ingredients:

- 1 russet potato (washed and scrubbed)
- 1 tbsp oil
- Kosher salt
- 2 bacon slices
- ¼ cup Cheddar cheese (shredded)
- Sour cream (to serve)
- Fresh chives (chopped, to serve, optional)

Directions:

Pierce the surface of the potato a few times with a fork.

Rub oil all over the skin of the potato and season with salt.

Place the potato on a microwave-safe plate along with the slices of bacon. Microwave on full power for 8 minutes or until the bacon is crisp and the potato is fork-tender. Don't allow the bacon to burn.

Remove from the microwave and allow the bacon to cool down slightly before crumbling. Set the bacon aside.

Cut the potato in half, and with a metal fork, fluff the inside.

Scatter shredded cheese over the top and return to the microwave for an additional 30 seconds.

Serve topped with sour cream, chives, and crumbled bacon.

Meat-Free Lasagna

A comforting and hearty pasta dish needn't contain any meat. It tastes just as good with a selection of Italian cheeses.

Servings: 1

Total Time: 12mins

Ingredients:

- ½ cup ricotta cheese
- ¼ cup fresh spinach (chopped)
- 2 tbsp fresh parsley (chopped)
- 2 tbsp Parmesan cheese (grated and divided)
- ½ tsp salt
- ¼ tsp black pepper
- ¼ cup store-bought marinara sauce
- 4 no-boil lasagna noodles (broken in half)
- ½ cup mozzarella cheese (shredded)

Directions:

In a bowl, combine the ricotta cheese with spinach, parsley, and 1 tablespoon Parmesan cheese. Season with salt and black pepper to taste.

In a glass container, spread an even layer of marinara sauce.

Add the noodles to the sauce and cover with an even layer of the ricotta cheese mixture. Next, top with the shredded mozzarella. Repeat the layering.

Cover the top layer of the noodles with additional marinara sauce and a layer of mozzarella and grated Parmesan.

Cover the glass container with a lid, but do not seal it closed.

Microwave on full power for 6-7 minutes, or until the cheese melts.

Carefully remove the lasagna from the microwave.

Set aside to cool.

Meatloaf in a Mug

If you are missing home-cooked meals, then discover how to recreate a traditional family meatloaf but this time in a mug.

Servings: 1

Total Time: 7mins

Ingredients:

- 2 tbsp 2% milk
- 1 tbsp ketchup
- 2 tbsp quick-cooking oats
- 1 tsp onion soup mix
- 4 ounces lean ground beef

Directions:

In a bowl, combine milk with ketchup, quick-cook oats, and onion soup mix.

Crumble the ground beef over the milk mixture, and mix thoroughly.

Transfer to a microwave-safe mug, and pat down gently.

Cover the mug and, on full power, cook for around 3 minutes, or until the meat registers an internal temperature of 160 degrees F. Drain well and set aside for 3 minutes to stand.

Serve and enjoy.

Mexican-Style Hotdogs

If you are burning the candle at both ends and fancy a fuss-free midnight snack, travel the south of the border and prepare these Mexican-style hotdogs.

Servings: 1

Total Time: 3mins

Ingredients:

- 2 tbsp Mexican bean mix
- 1 flour tortilla
- 1-2 ready-to-eat hot dogs
- 2 tbsp cheese (grated and divided)
- Salsa (as needed)

Optional Toppings:

- Dollop of sour cream (to serve)
- Dollop of guacamole (to serve)

Directions:

Spoon the Mexican bean mix down the center of a tortilla.

Add 1-2 ready-to-eat cooked hot dogs and top with half of the grated cheese.

Fold in the sides, and roll up burrito-style.

Add a spoonful or so of salsa followed by the remaining cheese.

Transfer to the microwave and cook on high for 45-60 seconds.

Enjoy with a dollop of sour cream and guacamole.

Microwave Pasta

Nothing could be simpler than this microwave Italian-style pasta dish.

Servings: 1

Total Time: 10mins

Ingredients:

- 2 ounces spaghetti (snap the strands in half)
- Salt (to season pasta water)
- 1¼ cups water (divided and as needed)
- ¼ tsp salt (or to taste)
- ½ tsp freshly ground black pepper
- 1 tbsp extra-virgin olive oil
- ¼ tsp dried Italian herbs
- ¼ cup Parmesan cheese (grated)

Directions:

Add the pasta to a microwave-safe bowl, laying it as flat as possible. Season with salt and 1 cup of water and gently shake from side to side to combine.

Uncovered, microwave on full power for 6-7 minutes, making sure the spaghetti doesn't dry out. If it looks like it may, you will need to add another ¼ cup of water, if necessary.

When 3 minutes, have elapsed break up any clumps of pasta. When a total of 6 minutes have elapsed, check that the pasta is al dente. Next, open the door of the microwave and allow the pasta to rest for 10 seconds.

When the spaghetti is al dente, there should be only around 1 tablespoon of liquid remaining. Do not drain, and instead stir in the salt, black pepper, oil, Italian herbs, and Parmesan cheese. Using a fork, toss to coat the spaghetti and serve.

Microwave Salmon

Meals created in the dorm aren't all about recreating fast-food favorites, and sometimes it's good to go the extra mile and prepare a healthy seafood meal for one.

Servings: 1

Total Time: 7mins

Ingredients:

- 1 (4-6 ounce) salmon fillet (rinsed and patted dry)
- Salt and freshly ground black pepper (to season)
- 2 tbsp mayonnaise
- 1-2 tbsp sriracha sauce (to taste)
- 2 lemon slices
- 1 tbsp parsley (chopped)

Directions:

Lay the salmon, skin side facing down in a microwave-safe container. Season the fish with salt and black pepper and put to one side.

In a bowl, combine the mayo with the sriracha sauce, according to taste.

Spread the mayo mixture evenly over the salmon, place the slices of lemon on top and scatter over the parsley.

Cover the container with microwave-friendly kitchen wrap and microwave for 3-4 minutes. Check for doneness, and if not cooked through, microwave for another 30-45 seconds.

Serve and enjoy.

Omelet in a Mug

Just because you are living in a college dorm needn't mean you can't eat healthy food, and this protein-packed omelet will get your brain working.

Servings: 1

Total Time: 3mins

Ingredients:

- 2 eggs
- ½ red or green bell pepper (diced)
- 2 ham slices (diced small)
- ¼ cup fresh spinach (chopped small)
- Salt and black pepper (to season)

Directions:

Add the eggs, bell pepper, ham, and spinach to a large microwave-safe mug. Season with salt and black pepper. With a fork, whisk to combine thoroughly.

Cook on full power for 2-3 minutes, without allowing the egg to bubble over.

Stir halfway through cooking.

Peanut Butter, Pear, Honey, and Cheese Open-Faced Sandwiches

The secret to a successful study snack is taste, texture, and speed. And these open-faced sandwiches with a sweet and savory topping are way better than anything you are likely to find in the cafeteria.

Servings: 2-4

Total Time: 2mins

Ingredients:

- ¼ cup crunchy peanut butter
- 4 honey whole wheat bread slices (toasted)
- 1 medium pear (cored and thinly sliced)
- ¼ tsp salt
- 4 tsp runny honey
- ½ cup Cheddar cheese (shredded)

Directions:

Spread the peanut butter evenly over the toasted bread.

Top with pear slices, honey, and shredded Cheddar cheese.

Place the open sandwiches on a microwave-safe plate and on high, cook for 20-25 seconds, until the cheese melts.

Potato Chips

If money is tight, then these homemade microwave potato chips will keep your snack cravings at bay.

Servings: 2

Total Time: 15mins

Ingredients:

- 1 russet potato (washed, scrubbed, dried, and cut into ⅛" slices)
- 2 tbsp olive oil
- Nonstick cooking spray (as needed)
- Sea salt (to season)
- Dip (of choice, to serve, optional)

Directions:

Pat the slices of potatoes with a kitchen paper towel until dry.

Transfer the potatoes to a ziplock bag and pour in the oil. Shake the bag to coat.

Spritz a large microwave-safe plate with nonstick cooking spray, and with kitchen paper, wipe the spray over the plate. This step will help to prevent the chips from sticking.

In batches and in a single layer, arrange the chips on the lightly greased plate and season with sea salt.

On high, microwave the chips until they are starting to brown, for around 5-10 minutes. Once the potato chips begin to develop a little color, take them out of the microwave and peel slowly off the plate.

Repeat the process until all the potato slices are cooked. There is no need to coat the plate in nonstick cooking oil again.

Serve with your favorite dip, and enjoy.

Red Curry Rice Noodles

Make sure you include this tasty meat-free recipe in your repertoire of dorm-friendly meals.

Servings: 1

Total Time: 5mins

Ingredients:

- ½ tbsp Thai red curry paste
- ½ cup coconut milk
- 1 portion rice vermicelli noodles
- 1-2 tbsp onion (peeled and chopped)
- 1 handful of frozen vegetables (of choice)
- 1-3 tbsp of water

Directions:

In a microwave-safe bowl, combine the red curry paste with coconut milk, and continue to mix until the paste is a thin consistency.

To the bowl, add the noodles, onion, and veggies. Stir to evenly and well coat the noodles. Add 1-3 tablespoons of water, depending on your preferred level of wetness.

Transfer the bowl to the microwave, and on full power, cook for around 3 minutes. Check on the doneness of noodles, and if not cooked, return to the microwave and cook in 30-second increments until good to go.

Serve and enjoy.

Shakshuka

They say that variety is the spice of life, and next time you are tired of bland dining hall food, eat smart and prepare this tasty North African-style dish.

Servings: 1

Total Time: 7mins

Ingredients:

- Nonstick cooking spray
- ¼ cup store-bought marinara sauce
- ¼ cup canned chickpeas (cooked, drained, and rinsed)
- ⅛ tsp red pepper flakes
- Pinch of kosher salt
- 1 egg
- Cilantro (chopped, to garnish, optional)

Directions:

Spritz a microwave-safe bowl with nonstick cooking spray.

To the bowl, add the marinara sauce, chickpeas, red pepper flakes, and season with salt. Stir the mixture well to combine.

Create a well in the middle of the sauce mixture. Break the egg into the well and pierce the center of the yolk with a sharp paring knife.

Cover the bowl with a damp kitchen paper towel. On 80 percent power, microwave for 60 seconds and continue to cook in 20-second increments, still on 80 percent power, until the egg white is set and the yolk is your preferred level of doneness. This process may take around 3-4 increments.

Garnish with chopped cilantro; if using, serve and enjoy.

Speedy Shrimp

There really is no excuse not to head straight for the microwave when you can prepare this boujee seafood dish for 4 in just 6 minutes.

Servings: 4

Total Time: 6mins

Ingredients:

- 2 tbsp butter
- 1 large garlic clove (peeled and minced)
- ⅛ -¼ tsp cayenne pepper (to taste)
- 2 tbsp white wine
- 5 tsp fresh lemon juice
- 1 tbsp fresh parsley (minced)
- ½ tsp salt
- 24-32 uncooked shrimps (peeled and deveined)

Directions:

Add the butter, garlic, and cayenne pepper, according to taste, to a 9" microwave-safe pie plate.

Cover and microwave on high for around 60 seconds until the butter melts.

Stir in the white wine, fresh lemon juice, parsley, and salt.

Add the shrimps to the mixture, and toss gently to coat.

Cover and on high, microwave until the shrimps are pink for 2½-3½ minutes.

Stir and serve.

Spinach and Cheddar Quiche in a Mug

This veggie-packed quiche is full of protein and the perfect meal in a mug to enjoy any time of the day or night.

Servings: 1

Total Time: 5mins

Ingredients:

- ½ cup packed fresh spinach
- 2 tbsp cold water
- 1 egg
- ⅓ cup milk
- ⅓ cup Cheddar cheese (shredded)
- 1 bacon slice (chopped)
- Salt and black pepper (to season)

Directions:

Add the fresh spinach to a microwave-safe mug along with 2 tablespoons of water. Cover with a kitchen paper towel and on high, microwave for 60 seconds. Remove the spinach from the microwave, drain the water and expel any water by squeezing.

Break the egg into the mug and pour in the milk. Add the shredded cheese and bacon. Season with salt and black pepper, mixing thoroughly to combine.

Cover with a kitchen paper towel, and on high, microwave for 3 minutes, or until cooked thoroughly.

Sweet 'n Sour Meatballs

If you are tired of campus food, no problem, head off to the dorm, and in just 10 minutes, you can be tucking into this Asian-inspired microwave dish.

Servings: 2

Total Time: 9mins

Ingredients:

- 8 fully-cooked frozen homestyle meatballs
- 1 medium carrot (trimmed and diced)
- ¼ small yellow onion (peeled and cut into small chunks)
- ½ small green pepper (julienned)
- 1 garlic clove (peeled and minced)
- ½ cup store-bought jarred sweet 'n sour sauce (any brand)
- 2 tsp soy sauce
- 1 cup rice (cooked and hot)

Directions:

Add the meatballs to a microwave-safe dish of 3-quart capacity.

Scatter over the diced carrot, onion, bell pepper, and minced garlic.

In a bowl, combine the sweet 'n sour sauce with the soy sauce. Pour the mixture over the meatball veggie mix.

Cover, and microwave on high for 6-8 minutes, until the meatballs are heated through and the veggies are bite-tender. You will need to stir twice during this process.

Serve the meatballs on a bed of rice.

Tuna Melt

It's official! Tuna is a valuable source of protein, and what's more, it is high in B12, niacin, and selenium, which means not only does it taste good, but it's also good for concentration.

Servings: 4

Total Time: 3mins

Ingredients:

- 4 bagels (split, to yield 8 halves)
- 2 (8 ounces) cans tuna in water or oil (drained)
- 8 American cheese slices

Directions:

Top each bagel half with an even amount of tuna.

Place a slice of American cheese on top of the tuna.

Two at a time, microwave the tuna and cheese-topped bagel halves for around 2 minutes, or until the cheese melts.

Serve and enjoy.

Desserts and Sweet Snacks

Apple Sponge Pudding

This fruity and fluffy apple mug sponge is both vegan and vegetarian-friendly!

Servings: 1

Total Time: 4mins

Ingredients:

- 1 tbsp superfine sugar
- 3 tbsp plain flour
- ¼ tsp ground cinnamon
- ½ tsp baking powder
- Pinch of kosher salt
- 1 tbsp oil
- 3 tbsp almond milk
- ¼ tsp vanilla extract
- 2 tbsp applesauce
- Custard (to serve)

Directions:

Combine the flour, sugar, baking powder, cinnamon, and salt in a bowl. Add the oil, almond milk, and vanilla and whisk to combine.

Pour the apple sauce into a large, microwave-safe mug and spoon over the sponge batter.

Cook in the microwave for 90 seconds on high heat. The sponge is ready if you can press it gently with your finger, and it springs back.

Serve with warmed custard if desired.

Banana and Peanut Butter Oatmeal

Are you suffering after a big night out? This wholesome dorm-friendly banana and peanut butter oatmeal with fiber-rich flax and chia seeds will get your mind, body, and soul back on track even after the wildest time!

Servings: 1

Total Time: 5mins

Ingredients:

- 1 ripe banana (peeled and mashed)
- ½ tsp chia seeds
- ½ tsp flax seeds
- ¼ tsp ground cinnamon
- 1 cup unsweetened almond milk
- ½ tbsp peanut butter

Directions:

In a large, microwave-safe bowl, stir together the mashed banana, chia seeds, flax seeds, cinnamon, and almond milk.

Place in the microwave, and on high heat, cook for 3-3½ minutes. Stir the oats every 90 seconds to ensure they do not spill over the bowl.

Take the oatmeal out of the microwave and immediately stir in the peanut butter.

Serve straight away and enjoy.

Carrot Mug Cake

No need for an oven and a multitude of baking tools. Just a humble mug and microwave are all it takes to whip up this delicious spicy carrot mug cake without even leaving your dorm.

Servings: 1

Total Time: 4mins

Ingredients:

- 2 tbsp granulated sugar
- 3 tbsp flour
- Pinch of ground cinnamon
- Pinch of ground allspice
- ½ tsp baking powder
- Pinch of kosher salt
- 2 tbsp sunflower oil
- 2 tbsp whole milk
- 1 carrot (peeled and grated)
- Greek yogurt (to serve, optional)

Directions:

Stir the sugar, flour, cinnamon, allspice, baking powder, and a pinch of salt in a large, microwave-safe mug.

Next, pour in the sunflower oil and milk and whisk with a fork. Finally, stir in the grated carrot.

Cook in the microwave for 90 seconds, but start to check the mug cake after 60 seconds to avoid overcooking.

Take out of the microwave, top with a spoonful of yogurt if desired, and serve immediately.

Cocoa Popcorn

Power through a study break and tuck into a big bowl of hot popcorn.

Servings: 1

Total Time: 3mins

Ingredients:

- 1½ tbsp popcorn kernels
- ½ tsp coconut oil
- ½ tsp cocoa powder
- ½ tsp sugar
- Pinch of salt

Directions:

Add the popcorn kernels to a brown bag. Fold the top of the bag over a few times.

Place the bag in the microwave and on high, cook for 60-90 seconds, until the kernels start to pop.

Add the coconut oil to a small microwave-safe bowl. Melt the oil in the microwave for around 20 seconds until melted. Using a fork, stir the oil.

Add the oil, cocoa, and sugar to the bag and over the popcorn. Season to taste with a pinch of salt, fold over the top of the brown bag, and shake to coat evenly.

French Toast in a Cup

If you are rushing off to classes in the morning, make sure you get off to a good start with this quick-to-prepare French toast in a cup.

Servings: 1

Total Time: 8mins

Ingredients:

- 1 tbsp butter
- 1-2 bread slices (cut into cubes)
- 1 egg
- 3 tbsp milk
- 1 dash of cinnamon
- 1-2 drops vanilla extract (to taste, optional)
- Syrup (as needed, to serve, optional)

Directions:

In a microwave-safe cup, in your microwave, melt the butter for 2-3 seconds. Then, swirl the melted butter around the mug.

Add the bread cubes to the cup.

In a second cup, combine the egg with milk, a dash of cinnamon, and 1-2 drops of vanilla extract to taste. Stir well to combine.

Pour the egg mixture over the bread, and swirl to soak the bread.

Transfer to the microwave for 60 seconds. After that, microwave in 10-second increments until cooked to your preferred level of doneness. Cooking time is around 80-90 seconds.

Drizzle with your favorite syrup and enjoy.

Golden Syrup Pudding

This self-saucing golden syrup pudding will bring a taste of home comfort to your dorm room.

Servings: 4

Total Time: 15mins

Ingredients:

- ¾ cup granulated sugar
- ½ cup whole milk
- 1 cup self-raising flour
- 4 tbsp butter (chopped)
- 3 tbsp golden syrup
- 1½ cups boiling water
- Pouring cream (to serve)

Directions:

In a microwave-safe dish, stir together the sugar, milk, and flour. Dot the chopped butter on top.

Dissolve the golden syrup in the boiling water in a mug and pour over the pudding mixture in the dish.

Cook the pudding in the microwave for 7-9 minutes on high heat.

Take the pudding out of the microwave and serve warm with lashings of cream.

Lemon Pudding

Not having a large kitchen space is no reason not to enjoy a tasty homemade pudding. This lemon pudding, "baked" in the microwave, is air-light and bursting with a fresh and zesty lemon flavor.

Servings: 4

Total Time: 5mins

Ingredients:

- 3½ ounces superfine sugar
- 3½ ounces self-raising flour
- 3½ ounces butter (at room temperature)
- 2 eggs
- 1 tsp vanilla extract
- Zest of 1 lemon
- 4 tbsp lemon curd
- Crème fraiche (to serve, optional)

Directions:

Whisk together the sugar, flour, butter, eggs, vanilla, and lemon zest in a bowl.

Transfer the cake batter to a microwave-safe dish. Cook in the microwave for 3 minutes on high heat. Turn the dish halfway through. The cake should be set entirely and risen.

Take out of the microwave and allow to stand for 60 seconds.

In the meantime, warm the lemon curd in the microwave for 30 seconds until a consistency that is easy to drizzle.

Pour the warm lemon curd over the cooked cake and serve with dollops of crème fraiche if desired.

Microwave Mint Fudge

Are you off to a dorm party? Be the best-loved guest and take along this mint chocolate fudge. Nobody will ever guess you made it in the microwave!

Servings: 64

Total Time: 1hr 15mins

Ingredients:

- 1 tsp butter (to grease)
- 3¾ cups powdered sugar
- ½ cup baking cocoa powder
- 3½ tbsp skim milk
- 7½ tbsp butter (at room temperature)
- 1 tsp vanilla extract
- ½ cup crème de menthe or mint flavor baking chips

Directions:

Line an 8" square baking tin with foil and grease with 1 tsp butter.

In a medium, microwave-safe bowl, stir together the powdered sugar and baking cocoa. Add the milk and butter. Do not stir.

Place the bowl in the microwave and cook for 2–2½ minutes on high heat. Stir at intervals until the mixture is smooth and melted.

Stir in the vanilla extract.

Spread the fudge mixture in the prepared baking tin and scatter over the baking chips.

Chill the fudge in the refrigerator for 60 minutes or until firm.

Use the foil to lift the fudge out of the tin, slice into 1" squares and serve.

Mug Donut

This microwaveable mug recipe will bring you all the flavor of a sweet jam-filled donut?! Yes, please!

Servings: 1

Total Time: 3mins

Ingredients:

- 2 tbsp butter
- 4 tbsp flour
- Yolk of 1 egg
- 2 tbsp granulated sugar
- 1 tbsp whole milk
- ½ tsp baking powder
- 1 tbsp raspberry or strawberry jam
- Cinnamon sugar (to garnish, optional)

Directions:

Add the butter to a large, microwave-safe mug. Melt in the microwave for 30 seconds.

Take the mug out of the microwave and whisk in the flour, egg yolk, sugar, milk, and baking powder. Spoon the jam into the middle of the batter.

Cook in the microwave for 45-60 seconds on high heat. The top of the sponge should feel firm.

Sprinkle over a pinch of cinnamon sugar, if desired, before serving.

Protein Brownies

Fresh from the microwave in just 60 seconds, these brownies are fudgy and gooey and protein-packed for extra energy.

Servings: 1-2

Total Time: 3mins

Ingredients:

- 1 (1¼ ounces) scoop chocolate protein powder
- 1 tbsp coconut flour
- 2 tbsp granulated sweetener (of choice)
- ½ tsp baking powder
- 1-2 tbsp cocoa powder (to taste)
- 1 large egg
- ¼ cup milk
- 1 tbsp chocolate chips

Directions:

In a microwave-safe bowl, combine the chocolate protein powder with coconut flour, baking powder, sweetener (to taste), baking powder, and cocoa powder (to taste). Mix thoroughly.

In a second bowl, whisk the egg with the milk and pour into the dry mixture and mix until combined. Scatter over the chocolate chips.

Microwave on high power for 60 seconds.

Pumpkin Pie Mug Cake

Are you feeling homesick? Then, why not enjoy all the familiar flavors of fall in a mug.

Servings: 1

Total Time: 6mins

Ingredients:

- 1 tsp unsalted butter
- 2 ginger snap cookies (crushed to yield 1 tablespoon of crumbs)
- ⅓ cup pumpkin puree
- 1 large egg
- 1 tbsp whole milk
- 2 tbsp packed brown sugar
- 1 tsp pumpkin pie spice

Directions:

Add the butter to a microwave-safe mug, and on low, microwave until melted.

Stir in the crushed cookies and press the mixture firmly into the bottom of the microwave-safe mug.

In a small bowl, whisk the pumpkin puree with egg, whole milk, pumpkin pie spice, and sugar. Transfer the mixture to the mug and over the gingersnap crust.

Set the mug on a microwave-safe plate.

On full power, microwave for 2-5 minutes, until a skewer pulls out clean when inserted into the middle of the pie. The best way to achieve a successful mug cake is to cook for 2 minutes and then in 30-second increments until cooked to your preference.

Remove from the microwave and enjoy.

Quick Apple Crisp

Are you inviting your classmates over to your dorm? Then, this sweet and simple-to-prepare apple crisp is the perfect treat to share.

Servings: 8

Total Time: 12mins

Ingredients:

- 1 cup crushed graham crackers
- ½ cup brown sugar
- ½ cup all-purpose flour
- 1 tsp ground cinnamon
- ½ tsp ground nutmeg
- ½ cup butter (melted)
- Butter (to grease)
- 8 tart apples (peeled, cored, and sliced)
- Whipped cream (to serve)

Directions:

Combine the crushed crackers, brown sugar, flour, cinnamon, nutmeg, and melted butter in a bowl.

Grease a 2½-quart microwave-safe dish with butter. Add the apple slices to the dish and scatter over the cracker mixture.

Place in the microwave and cook for 8-9 minutes, until the apples are tender.

Divide the dessert between serving bowls and top each portion with a dollop of whipped cream.

Enjoy!

Red Velvet Cake in a Mug

Tangy cream cheese frosting is the perfect finishing touch to this soft and fluffy red velvet cake, which, you guessed it, is "baked" in a humble microwave-safe mug.

Servings: 1

Total Time: 35mins

Ingredients:

Cake:

- 2 tbsp granulated sugar
- 4 tbsp all-purpose flour
- ⅛ tsp bicarbonate of soda
- ½ tbsp unsweetened cocoa powder
- 2 tbsp buttermilk
- ½ tbsp vegetable oil
- 1 tbsp skim milk
- ⅛ tsp vinegar
- ¼ tsp red food coloring

Frosting:

- ½ ounce cream cheese
- ½ ounce butter
- 2-3 tbsp powdered sugar

Directions:

In a large, microwave-safe mug, add all the ingredients (sugar, flour, bicarb, cocoa powder, buttermilk, oil, milk, vinegar, and red food coloring) and whisk together using a fork until smooth.

Cook on high heat in the microwave for 60 seconds.

Take the cake out of the microwave and allow to rest for 30 minutes.

In the meantime, prepare the frosting. Beat together the cream cheese, butter, and powdered sugar to create a fluffy frosting. The amount of powdered sugar will depend on your preferred consistency, so begin by adding 2 tablespoons.

Spread the prepared frosting over the cooled cake before serving.

Strawberry 'n Cream Mug Cake

When you are away from those you love and craving cake, there's no need to waste food and time buying or baking a whole sponge. Instead, make this super scrumptious single-serving treat in under 10 minutes.

Servings: 1

Total Time: 6mins

Ingredients:

- 4 tbsp flour
- 3 tbsp granulated sugar
- ½ tsp baking powder
- 2 fresh strawberries (hulled and diced)
- 3 tbsp whole milk
- 1 tbsp oil
- 1 tsp vanilla extract
- Vanilla ice cream (to serve)

Directions:

In a large, microwave-safe mug, stir together all of the ingredients (flour, sugar, baking powder, strawberries, milk, oil, and vanilla extract) until combined.

Cook in the microwave for 1½-2 minutes on high heat. Keep a close eye to make sure the batter doesn't bubble over.

Take the cake out of the microwave and allow it to rest for 60 seconds.

Top with ice cream if desired and serve.

Vanilla Cheesecake

This sweet dessert will satisfy those sweet cravings, and more importantly, it's kind on the food budget and delicious. It's a 'berry' nice sweet treat!

Servings: 1

Total Time: 40mins

Ingredients:

- 1 tbsp butter
- 2 graham cracker sheets (crushed into crumbs)
- 2 tbsp sugar
- 4 ounces cream cheese (softened)
- 3 drops vanilla extract
- 4 fresh berries (of choice, to serve)

Directions:

In a small microwave-safe ramekin, melt the butter. Swirl the ramekin to coat.

Add the cracker crumbs to the melted butter, and mix thoroughly. Using a spoon, press the crackers evenly against the bottom of the ramekin.

Combine the sugar, cream cheese, and vanilla extract in a small bowl, stirring well until lump-free.

Spread the filling evenly over the top of the cracker crust.

Transfer the ramekin to the microwave and cook at 50 percent power, for a minimum of 4 minutes, in 45-second increments. Do not allow the cheesecake to bubble over the ramekin's sides.

Remove from the microwave. Then, transfer to the freezer to chill for a minimum of 30 minutes, or until cool to the touch.

Loosen the edges of the cheesecake with a knife, invert onto a plate, top with fresh berries, and enjoy.

Afterword

You finished this book and read it all to this point. To be honest, there's no way I can show you how much I appreciate you. You took the time out of your very busy life to stare at my thoughts that I put into words, thank you. You've already done enough but I still have one more favor to ask of you, feedback. I would love to know what you think about this book's content; did you enjoy it? Was it worth your time? Do you have any suggestions for future books? I'm open to comments and I'll love to hear from you.

Thank you again

Matthew Goods

About the Author

Known as the boy wonder of Homemade cuisine, he has been dubbed the "Jack of all Spices". Born in a small town in South Carolina, Matthew Goods was a local boy who, at a very early age of 7 had found a hobby that will stick with him for the rest of his life in the culinary arts. He loved being in and around the kitchen whenever his mother late.

This meant Matthew spent most of his free time after school alone, and he filled this time by experimenting with different mixes, ingredients, and spices and by the time he was 15, he was already a budding chef at one of the best-rated restaurants in the town. After traveling around the world for over a decade, working at various levels of restaurants, Goods now runs a successful restaurant that serves his special recipes where he is the executive chef.

Made in United States
Troutdale, OR
12/18/2023

16046413R00053